The Case of the Prickly Feelings

Lynne Namka, Ed. D.

Illustrated by Scott Nelson

Talk, Trust and Feel Therapeutics

Tucson, Arizona

Also by Lynne Namka

Self-Help Books

The Doormat Syndrome
How to Let Go of Your Mad Baggage
Avoiding Relapse: Catching Your Inner Con
A Gathering of Grandmothers: Words of
Wisdom from Women of Spirit and Power
Your Quick Anger Makeover: Plus Twenty Cutting-Edge Techniques to Release Anger!

Children's Books

The Mad Family Gets Their Mads Out
Good Bye Ouchies and Grouchies, Hello Happy Feelings: EFT for Kids of All Ages
Teaching Emotional Intelligence to Children: Fifty Fun Activities for Families and Therapists
Parents Fight Parents Make Up: Take Good Care of Yourself

Fiction

Love as a Fine Species of Madness
Castalia Every After
The Loathsome Lady: The Marriage of Sir Gawain and Dame Ragnell

Books are available at angriesout.com and Amazon.com

Published by Talk, Trust and Feel Therapeutics
5398 E. Golder Ranch Drive, Tucson, AZ 85739

"Big feelings! Little feelings!
Okay. Okay.
You have some anger, sadness or other unhappy feelings.
It's normal to have all kinds of feelings, even bad ones.
Feelings are for learning.
You can learn a lot about yourself by watching your feelings.

Take your feelings seriously.
Feelings are meant to be felt, understood, explored and then released.
Hang out with your feelings and see what they have to tell you.
They provide signals that hold information for you.
It's what you do with your feelings that count."

Lynne Namka   How to Let Go of Your Mad Baggage

Bummer. Things were not going well. I had been out of sorts all week. Grumpy and grouchy. Things were all jumbled up inside.

My best friend Mac was mad at me. My sister Janie had tattled on me twice. I was grounded. Twice!

Something had been puzzling me. Something was missing. I couldn't quite put my finger on it.

I decided to write some notes in my journal.

It all started when my teacher Mrs. Young talked about feelings. She asked me how I felt about getting a bad grade on my math test. I told her that I feel like I need to understand fractions better. Mrs. Young agreed but said that wasn't really a feeling. She told me I needed to learn about real feelings.

Feelings! I puzzled over it but couldn't figure it out. What is a feeling? I just didn't get it.

I whispered to my friend, Mac McGregor, "Mac, what is a feeling?"

Mac shook his head. "I dunno. Will this class never end? I feel like it's time to go play ball. I wish it was recess time."

Huh? That didn't seem right. That was more like wishes not real feelings. Well, what do dogs know about feelings, anyway? They are happy most of the time.

There must be clues about feelings. I decided to search for the clues. I wrote on my notebook in big letters: Feelings are not wishes or things that you want to do.

CLUES ABOUT FEELINGS

Feelings aren't wishes or things you want to do.

After school I ran home and hollered at my sister, "Hey Janie, what's a feeling?"

Janie didn't even look up as she said, "I feel like I'm going to come out of my skin if you bug me one more time. I feel like I've had it with you."

Her answer didn't fit with what my teacher had said. Not what I was looking for, but maybe it's a clue. When somebody says, "I feel like….," it is probably not a real feeling.

I thought about how Janie had been annoyed with me recently. I'd been grumpy. I bet annoyed and grumpy are feelings. I got my notebook and wrote the latest clue in big letters.

CLUES ABOUT FEELINGS

When someone says, "I feel like…," it's not a feeling.

I went to find Mom who was surfing the web. "What's a feeling? We talked about feelings at school. I'm looking for clues to understand feelings."

Mom mumbled, "Mmmm, I don't know, Jake. It's something you feel. You know, feel. Go get the dictionary and look it up."

I flipped through the dictionary to search for the word. "The dictionary doesn't help." I said, "It says, full of emotion and a bunch of stuff that don't make sense."

"Well, don't ask your dad," mom said. "He doesn't have a clue as to what a feeling is unless he gets mad. Why don't you go ask Grandma? She was a counselor before she retired. She'll know what feelings are."

Great idea! I ran to get my detective hat.

The folks at my house seemed so prickly all the time. I wonder if prickly is a feeling. If it is, we've got lots of it at our house.

Well, I'm a detective and this is my case. Detective Jake, that's me. I'm on the search to get clues to figure out feelings. I had to get the facts, just the facts about feelings.

I got out my notebook and went over what I had written. I'll keep looking for clues about feelings. There has t to be clues that will help me solve this case.

Grandma met me with a big welcoming smile. I have to tell you that she's a weird kind of grandmother. She isn't the usual kind of bake-you-cookies kind of grandma. Or the let's-go-to-the-mall-and-shop kind of grandma. She listens to you and does fun things. She is a let's have-a-squirt-bottle-water-fight grandma.

"Come on in. I'm just making some tea. How about some weed tea?" she said.

As I said, she was a strange kind of grandma. She picked weeds from her garden to make tea.

I tried hard to keep from making a face. "No thank you," I said using my best manners voice. Grandma let me tease her about her being different in a good way. "Grandma, you're weird. Weird. Good weird, but weird."

"Takes one to know one! Just the right amount of weird, I hope." We laughed over our old joke. Actually I liked that she was a funny kind of grandma.

"What's up with you today? You look kind of puzzled."

I touched my hat and said in my deepest voice, "I'm Detective Jake. I'm here on a case. I'm looking for clues about feelings. The facts, Ma'am. I just want the facts. And clues. The folks at my house don't seem to know what feelings are."

Grandma smiled, "You've got that right. Many grownups don't understand feelings."

I nodded and rolled my eyes. "Yeah! My parents and Jamie are prickly a lot. I'm beginning to wonder if we are a prickly family."

Grandma laughed so hard that her belly shook. "It's marvelous that you figured that out. Well, we are hedgehogs and hedgehogs are prickly and spiky creatures, you know. We do bristle at each other."

"Do we have to be so cross with each other all the time? You aren't prickly."

"That's because I've studied unhappy feelings and how to take care of them," she said. "I decided that I didn't want to be angry with people I cared about. Feelings are tricky. Some folks deal with their negative feelings by denying them. They ignore uncomfortable feelings that make them feel tense and weak. Some allow themselves only one feeling and that's anger. They get mad at people who criticize them or ask them to take responsibility for what they do wrong. They use anger to get others to back off so they won't feel bad."

I thought about how my dad got angry when he didn't want to answer my questions. "Dad sure can be roaring prickly at times. Especially when he doesn't want to hear what I have to say. He can't stand to be criticized."

"Being criticized about what they have done wrong makes some people defensive. When they feel guilty, they get angry to make others leave them alone. Some people substitute anger for other unwanted feelings. Do you know anything about that?"

I hated to admit it but I blew up at Janie when she asked me if I had borrowed her phone and I had.

Grandma looked at me over her glasses. "Feelings connect us to the world around us. They give us needed information. Our feelings make sense of what happens to us and help us decide how to act. They're complicated but when you understand the rules about working with them, you can figure them out. Then life becomes much easier."

"What are the rules? I want to write them down in my clue list."

"More people today are figuring out how to deal with their feelings, even the scary, strong ones like anger. When I was little, my parents didn't have a clue about feelings. Here's what helped me learn about them. Feelings are sad, mad, bad, glad and scad. Scad is a made-up word for scared. Other feelings are disappointed, bored, irritable, jealous and delighted. Or you might feel bored, upset, stubborn or confused. You are feeling one of these feelings right now. Confused. Right?"

Grandma could always tell what was up with me. I nodded. "What's the big deal with feelings? My teacher said it's a good idea to be in touch with your feelings. How can I touch a feeling if I don't even know what it is?"

"When something important happens, there's usually a feeling hiding underneath it. There are many different feelings and you can figure them out. Like now. How did you feel when I answered the door? Let a feeling come up."

I smiled remembering Grandma's face lighting up when she opened the door. "I feel happy when I see you."

"Likewise. Now think of a time when something went wrong. There's usually a feeling or two hiding there when you don't get what you want."

I thought of the fight I had with my friend. "Mac won't play with me. He's hardly even talking to me," I said. Suddenly I felt bad all over. "Oh, I just had another feeling. I felt bad!"

"Catching a feeling when it happens is the first step. Name it and tame it is the second step. Call that feeling out and give it a name like you just did. You can let go of some bad feelings by talking them through. Tell me about what's going on with you and Mac."

"We yelled at each other about the rules of the video game. I got mad and went home."

Grandma said, "Catching a feeling when it happens is the first step. Name it and tame it is the second step. Call that feeling out and give it a name like you just did. Tell me about what's going on with you and Mac. You can let go of some bad feelings by talking them through."

"Share your feelings to get them out so they don't get stuffed down inside. To get your feelings out, it helps to find someone safe who can listen to you."

Clues! I was getting more evidence about feelings. Here were more suggestions about what to do with unhappy feelings:

CLUES TO RELEASE PRICKLY FEELINGS

I can learn ways to let unhappy feelings go.

Catch a feeling when it comes up.

Give it a name. Name it and tame it!

Don't stuff unhappy feelings down.

Share upset feelings with someone safe.

"We get all kinds of feelings when people we care about get angry with us," she said. "It's normal to have powerful feelings. It's what you do with those feelings that count."

Yeah! I knew about strong feelings for sure. Especially the prickly, angry kind.

"One clue in understanding feelings is to see where your body is tense," Grandma continued. "Check your tummy, your chest, the back of your neck and even your hands. See what's happening inside. Think of the fight and let a feeling come out."

I noticed that my hands were tight and wanted to curl up into fists. "Frustrated. Kind of mad. Hey, I'm getting the hang of this feelings thing."

"Most people feel angry during a fight. Your hands look like they might want to hit someone. Remember; when you are upset to use your words instead of your fists. You can tell someone how you feel. Stick to feelings and stay away from name calling. It makes things worse when you take feelings out on others. Calling someone a name makes them angrier. Think about it."

"Sure, I get it. The fight got worse when I called Mac a cheese head."

Grandma's eyes twinkled. "Well no wonder! Would you like to be called a cheese head? Here is one thing to do to release the tightness in your fists. Breathe into your fists. Breathe deeply until the tension goes away. Let a feeling come up. Feelings come in layers. Take a big breath and let your angry feeling go."

I followed her instructions. Suddenly the anger shifted and a bunch of different feelings came up. "I'm feeling sad. And hurt. And bad."

"You've got a lot of different feelings all right. It's okay to feel unhappy when bad things happen. You have a right to your feelings. You can't keep feelings from coming. They come up all the time. That's what feelings do. It's what you do with your feelings that count. If you push them down inside or dwell on them, you'll keep on feeling bad. Better jot all that down." She repeated what she had said slowly.

CLUES TO RELEASE PRICKLY FEELINGS

I have a right to my feelings.

I check my body to see where the feelings hide.

Don't take bad feelings out on others or myself.

Venting anger and calling names makes me feel worse.

It's natural to feel unhappy when bad things happen.

Bad feelings aren't fun to keep around.

Look for a tight place in your body and breathe into it.

"Whew! It's complicated. No wonder people don't understand feelings. Grandma, sometimes I get in a bad mood and stay stuck there."

"Moods are changeable. The key to change is to be open minded and try new ways to work with your feelings." She looked sad. "Some people won't try new things that could help them be happier. How about it? Are you open to change?"

"Sure, I'm sick of feeling grouchy. It's no fun."

Grandma smiled crinkling up her eyes. "I know what we can do to let grouchy feelings go. Feelings are energy that wants to move. We'll use our feeling-moving tools. It's good to have several tools in your tool kit when you have a big job to do. Want to go for it?"

She waited until I agreed, giving her a High Five.

"First things first. Let's do some Self Talk words that you say to calm yourself down. Using positive words when you are upset helps you be in charge. You can always tell yourself to chill out. Here are some Self Talk words to say to feel better. Say this after me:"

After each line she stopped so I could say the words out loud myself.

"It's a feeling.
It's only a feeling.
Feelings are meant to be felt.
That's why they are called feelings.

Bad feelings don't want to stick around.
They want to go somewhere else.
So I'll give this feeling a name and feel it for a bit.
And do something to let it go.
I'll use Self Talk to soothe myself and calm myself down.

I'm a wonderful person with feelings and that's a marvelous thing to be!"

Remembering that it was okay to be someone with feelings made me feel better.

Grandma said. "Let's use another feeling-moving tool. Name a feeling you want to release and think of some nifty tool to use."

"It's no fun being angry at Mac," I said. "Let's do Magic Fingers and tap on our faces to calm ourselves down."

She laughed because Magic Fingers was her favorite tool to use with feelings. We'd played this game before.

I rubbed my fingers together and blew on them for good luck. I thought about the fight with Mac and started tapping across my head and down my face and neck. I tapped down the inside of my arms and back up again and then across my chest.

"Keep thinking of why you feel bad while you tap," said Grandma as she tapped along with me. "Tapping is a great tool for chasing bad feelings away. Tapping on your face and body helps you relax. I've got some of those same kind of feelings myself that I want to get out."

I felt better already. Magic Fingers works! I wrote down the new clues.

CLUES TO RELEASE PRICKLY FEELINGS

Feelings are meant to be felt.

Bad feelings are stuck energy that wants to move.

I'm open to new ways of releasing feelings.

I can learn to self-soothe when I'm upset.

I remind myself to chill out and calm down.

Use a feeling-moving tool to release bad feelings.

Magic Fingers helps relax my body and let things go.

"Grandma," I said. "We forgot the huff and puff part."

"Right-o," she laughed. "Let's huff and puff and breathe those bad feelings out. The breath is your friend when you are having a bad-feeling day. Your clever breath is always there ready to blow bad feelings away. Sads, mads, bads and scads don't stand a chance of hanging around when you use your magic fingers and blow them out with your huff-and-puff breath. What feeling do you want to release now?"

"I'm kind of disappointed in myself for getting so mad at Mac," I replied.

Grandma said, "Disappointment is a feeling we get when we don't get our way or when we do something we're not proud of. It's a normal feeling that can be released just like all others. Tell yourself that you can learn from this and move on. Forgiving yourself helps if you have learned your lesson and made the decision not to do the same thing again."

I took several deep breaths and huffed and puffed while I thought about blowing disappointment out. I was definitely starting to feel better.

"Now where do you want to send those unwanted feelings? Use your wild imagination and think of the farthest place you can think of."

I thought and thought. What was the farthest place I'd ever heard of? "I know! I know! Let's send them to a distant galaxy far, far away!"

I closed my eyes and imagined sending my mad, sad and bad feelings in a space capsule to that distant galaxy. I laughed again. It was fun to send those feeling so far away.

"That's right. Let your happy feelings transform those bad ones. Now check to see if you still have bad feelings."

"Just a moment." I wrote down the clue about imagining packing up all the bad feelings and sending them away.

I thought about the fight between Mac and me. I couldn't come up with a single bad feeling. "Grandma, they are gone! Now I know what feelings are and how to release them."

The case was solved! They had been found, named and sent packing!

CLUES TO RELEASE PRICKLY FEELINGS

I breathe into any unhappy feeling.

Huffing and puffing helps release
negative feelings.

Forgiving myself helps if I learn my
lesson and decide not to act that way
again.

I imagine packing up those feelings
and
sending them off to a safe place.

Grandma laughed and gave me a big hug. "You got it! Feelings come and feelings go. They will move if you do something positive to release them. Jot this one down: "I'm in charge of my feelings, not the other way around."

She looked over my shoulder to see the newest clues on my list.

"That's marvelous," Grandma said. "You are marvelous. Now there is one more thing. Tell yourself that you are a wonderful person with feelings and that's a marvelous thing to be!"

CLUES TO RELEASE PRICKLY FEELINGS

I'm in charge of my unhappy feelings;
they are
not in charge of me.

Now I can get back to my happy mood.

I'm a person with feelings and
that's a marvelous thing to be!

Helping Your Child with Unwanted Feelings

One important clue to being an effective parent or teacher is to work yourself out of a job by teaching your youngsters to be responsible and to work with their unruly feelings.

Self Talk will help your child remember ways to handle his or her feelings during challenging situations. Self Talk is part of the Cognitive Behavioral Therapy approach that works with the mind to change how things are perceived. Seeing things differently helps redirect negative emotions. Making choices and hearing your own voice helps cement new learnings. Teach your child to say Self Talk words out loud and his or her self-esteem will improve.

Model Self Talk for him by talking to yourself out loud when you are upset so your child can overhear you! For example you might say, "I'm feeling overwhelmed and upset right now. I'm going to go take a Time Out in my room for a few minutes and do some deep breathing and tapping to calm myself down."

Clues to Release Unwanted Feelings

Feelings come and go. Feelings are signals from your mind and body to give you information.

It's okay to feel unhappy or angry when something bad happens. You have a right to your feelings.

It's not okay to take your angry feelings out on yourself or someone else.

Feelings are meant to be felt, understood and handled.

You'll be a happier person if you learn to own your feelings and manage them.

Don't stuff feelings down. Talk them out with someone safe.

Feelings stack up. Look for other feelings hiding under your first one. Keep looking!

Your breath is your friend when you have a case of unwanted feelings. Breathe into any tight place in your body to chase bad feelings out.

Use your feeling-moving tools to make unwanted feelings go away quicker.

Use Self Talk to talk yourself down when you feel upset.

Use your Magic Fingers to tap on your face and body and breathe to calm yourself.

Use your wild imagination to make pictures in your mind to send bad feelings far, far away. Be in charge of your feelings, not the other way around!

Cues to Say to Angry Children
(A twinkle in your eye will help this go easier!)

Don't scold when your child becomes frustrated and upset.
Frustration is a normal emotion when something goes wrong.
Teach your child how to work with his or her frustration and
anger. Give information as to what you want your child to do
next. Give two or three choices to break into the energy of anger
and refocus the mind into problem solving. Ask questions that
cause your child to think—this will break into his or her
frustration and anger.

Asking your child to move into thinking and problem solving
when annoyed will shift him or her into the frontal part of the
brain that is logical and rational! If your child can't figure out what
to do, cue him by giving several options. Then ask him or her to
repeat what you said.

- Notice how hot you are getting. Are there some Self Talk
  words you could say?

- What could you say right now to soothe yourself?

- It looks as if you are getting upset with yourself. Tell
  yourself, "I breathe when I'm mad."

- Stop and think what you could say to yourself to become calmer.

- You look frustrated. What can you do with these feelings?

- You have a decision: Get yourself together or go to time out and get your mads under control. (Somehow the use of the words "mads" makes angry feelings acceptable to children.)

- Thanks for catching yourself when you felt like hitting. Good choice! Look at your fists. What do you do now?

- Do yourself a favor. Look at what you are doing right now. Do you like what's happening? What could you say to yourself to feel better?

- What's a better choice to do with your disappointment because you didn't get your way?

About the Author

Dr. Lynne Namka is a happy psychologist in private practice in Tucson, Arizona. She is an educator who teaches children and adults to learn ways to work with their feelings. She has published many books on feelings, anger management and healthy living and created lesson plans and kits to teach social skills to children. Her ideas in this book have been field tested with hundreds of angry children. See her award-winning Web site at www.angriesout.com for articles and Flash Videos on anger management, bullying, narcissism, domestic violence and skills for being in loving relationships. YouTube also has her Flash Videos on bullying and anger management for children.

About the Artist

Scott Nelson has been a full time freelance illustrator, cartoonist and author since 1987. His humorous, whimsical and colorful artwork has been distributed by all the major greeting card publishers in the USA and U.K. His children's book artwork has been featured by numerous well known publishers and his own authored illustrated book Mulch the Lawn mower received top honors in the Moms Choice Awards 2005. Visit his web site at www.ScottNelsonandSon.com.

Date_____ Email _____

Phone _____ Purchase Number _____

Ordered by:	Ship To:

QTY	TITLE	EA. PRICE	TOTAL
	Interactive CD-ROM "Get Your Angries Out"	$19.95	
	Curriculums		
	I Stop My Bully Behavior Curriculum, manual & toys	$89.95	
	Manual only—I Stop My Bully Behavior	$39.95	
	The Anger Works Kit – Curriculum, manual, toys (for Therapists & Counselors)	$79.95	
	Manual only—The Anger Works Kit (for Therapists & Counselors only)	$35.00	
	Time Out Kit Curriculum, manual & toys	$34.95	
	Children's Books		
	How to Let Go of Your Mad Baggage Half Price Sale! (Reg. $9.95)	$4.98	
	The Mad Family Gets Their Mads Out (buy from Amazon.com)	$9.95	
	Good Bye Ouchies and Grouchies, Hello Happy Feelings	$9.95	
	Teaching Emotional Intelligence to Children	$9.95	
	Parents Fight Parents Make Up—Take Good Care Half Price Sale!	$4.98	
	Adult Books		
	A Gathering of Grandmothers: Words Of Wisdom	$15.95	
	The Doormat Syndrome	$12.95	
	Avoiding Relapse: Catching Your Inner Con	$11.95	
	The Quick Anger Make Over	$19.95	
	Best Deals on Books		
	<u>Combo</u> Ouchies & Grouchies & Teaching Emotional Intelligence to Children	$18.95	
	<u>2some</u> Quick Anger Make Over and Parents Fight, Parents Make Up	$21.95	
	Free Gift! Parents Fight Parents Make (on orders over $75.00)	Free	

	Subtotal	
IF you live in Arizona add 7% tax		
Shipping & Handling		
TOTAL		

Talk, Trust & Feel Therapeutics
5398 Golder Ranch Road, Tucson, AZ 85739

SHIPPING AND HANDLING sent via U.S. Post Office Parcel Post

# of Books	U.S. P. O. Media Mail Shipping & Handling Charges	Canadian Shipping & Handling Charges [U.S. Funds only]
1	$4.75	$6.50
2 - 3	$5.50	$8.50
4 - 5	$6.50	$10.50
6 - 7	$7.80	$12.50
8 - 9	$8.20	$11.50
10 - 14	$8.50	$13.00
15	$10.00	$15.00

For foreign orders, we suggest your purchasing our books in e-book form at

http://timetoloveyourself.com/Lynne_Namka_Products.html

This is my daughter Karen's online book store where my writings are sold as Adobe Acrobat book to download at a lower price at
www.timetoloveyourself.com/

Amazom.com has several of my books available as Kindle or paperback copies.

www.amazon.com/Lynne-Namka/e/B001K8R9M8

Make all checks payable to Talk, Trust & Feel Therapeutics.

Sorry, we cannot accept email, FAX or credit card orders.

Discounts for large orders for Therapists, Schools and Workshop Leaders

SELL OUR CHILDREN'S BOOKS AND THE CD!

Distributors and Schools: attach a Purchase Order number to order form and we'll ship and invoice as instructed.

We hope our products which teach responsibility and love in action help you and your children!

☺ Thank you for your order! ☺

Kids, parents, teachers and therapists can visit www.angriesout.com for many articles about anger and a form for ordering books, lesson plans and kits.

I'm a wonderful being with feelings and that's a
marvelous thing to be!

31300062R00031

Made in the USA
Middletown, DE
30 December 2018